FALLEN STARS1

CONTENTS

Fallen Stars 1
©Canfora Publishing 2018
ISBN: 978-91-984775-0-4
Design: Toni Canfora
Print: Printall, Estonia

Canfora Publishing / Canfora Grafisk Form
Upplandsgatan 96A
113 44 Stockholm, Sweden
www.canfora.se

INTRODUCTION

The editor and I were working out the details to bring my "Grounded Eagles" and "Setting Suns" series of photo-studies on captured and wrecked Axis aircraft back into print. I mentioned that over the years of collecting images for those books, I had acquired many photos of USAAF aircraft in various forms of distress. "I'd love to see them," Toni replied. I pulled together the files and sent them to Sweden.

Shortly afterwards, "Fallen Stars" was born. For both Toni and I, the hardest part of this project was choosing between the images. For each one we selected, there were at least two that didn't make the cut. The good news is, we have more to continue the series. We are already in the process of doing so.

American airmen and the Signal Corps took excellent photos of their warbirds. Benefiting from those collections, we've been able to cover almost every major USAAF combat aircraft type in this first volume of Fallen Stars. Modelers, historians, and the legions of WWII aircraft enthusiasts will enjoy these images, and the incredible details they contain. These are compelling photos of remarkable aircraft in unique situations.

The men and machines of the USAAF were able to overcome the many challenges presented by Mother Nature in addition to those presented by their Axis opponents in global, aerial combat. The greatest generation of aviation was certainly at its best when things were the worst. The photographic evidence of their courage and sacrifice is presented here for your review.

For their help in the preparation of this book, I would like to thank the kind men and women of the National Archives and the US Air Force Historical Research Agency, USAAF veterans Elmer Pankratz and Marty Richards, the Military History Society of Rochester, Bob Coalter and the Army Air Corps Museum, and of course, Toni Canfora. My love and thanks go to my friends, family and my wife Jennifer.

Tom Laemlein

The revenge of General Mud: P-38 Lightning towed out of the muck by a M2 High-Speed Tractor, made by the Cleveland Tractor Company, commonly known as a "Cletrac". France, December 1944.

Not covered in snow, but rather in flame-retardant foam. Belly-landed P-38 of the 2nd Service Group in Iceland, February 1944.

A 5th Air Force P-38 "Elsie" snapped its nose gear on landing at Dobodura, New Guinea during April 1943. The Lightning's tricycle landing gear could be a problem on rough airstrips.

"Miss Virginia" of the 339th Fighter Squadron, crash-landed at Guadalcanal after the mission to intercept Japanese Admiral Yamamoto. April 18, 1943.

Nose job: P-38 salvaged in Solomon Islands.

Left page, top:

Jungle wreck: A P-38 of the 10th Air Force, come to grief in India during the summer of 1945.

Left page, bottom:

Arctic salvage: wrecked P-38s of the 344th Fighter Squadron on Shemya Island, in the Aleutian Islands chain.

There are many hazards in the combat zone: this P-38 was destroyed when its brakes failed. Fortunately, the pilot was saved. Middleburg Island, August 1944.

Left page:
The Pacific Theater was designated second in the USAAF supply and logistics chain. Thus, any usable parts were removed from wrecked aircraft. Here the wreck of a P-38 gets picked over, Vella Lavella, October 1943.

Nosed over with its front gear snapped, this Bell P-39 Airacobra awaits recovery on rough strip near Nome, Alaska in the autumn of 1942.

Left page:
Airacobra overhaul: mechanics install a new Allison V-1710 engine. Note the details of the rear-mounted engine, cockpit and weapons bay in the nose. Townsville, Australia, June 1943.

Door Art: "My Gal Sal III" shows off the unusual car-door of the P-39 Airacobra. SW Pacific, 1943.

A Bell P-400 (the export version of the P-39), originally sent to England, and returned to the USAAF. This aircraft retains hints of its original British camouflage. Note the 20mm Hispano cannon in the nose (replacing the normal 37mm gun in US Airacobras). Port Moresby, New Guinea during January 1943.

"Pranged" but repairable. Men of the 2nd Air Base Group work to clear the runway of a crashed P-40B. Iceland, April 1942.

Left page:
Men of the 2nd Service Group salvage parts from a P-40E, crashed in Iceland during August 1943. Note the simple gunsight mounted outside the cockpit.

Even simple operations in extreme weather areas had their dangers. A P-40B off the runway in Iceland during February 1943.

Not every aircraft made it to the combat zone: this P-40F of the 45th Ferrying Squadron crashed on its way to a forward airfield. Algeria, February 1943.

Left page, top:
Air raid victim: Curtiss P-40 bombed and burnt out at Dinjan Field, India during October 1942.

Left page, bottom:
"War Weary" was worn out as a US combat aircraft and was being retired to a Chinese training squadron. The P-40 crashed landed during the ferry flight to its new base. Kunming, China, April 1944.

Above:
A P-40K of 14th Air Force, crashed at a Chinese base during November 1944. Note the details of its Allison engine.

Above:
Icelandic Thunderbolt: P-47D of the 2nd Service Group crash landed at Meeks Field in Iceland during June 1944.

Right page, top:
Ground pounder: this P-47 of the XXIX Tactical Air Command (supporting the US 9th Army) flipped on take-off. The pilot was only slightly injured but had to be dug out of his cockpit immersed in the mud.

Right page, bottom:
US combat engineers rescue a crashed P-47 at St. Laurent Sur Mer in the summer of 1944.

"Stinky Poo!", a P-47 of the 353rd Fighter Group, after a bad landing in England, October 1943.

"SNAFU": A razorback Thunderbolt of 78th Fighter Group, bellied in at Duxford, England during December 1944.

P-47 of 386ᵗʰ Fighter Squadron, shown after being recovered from the water off "Juno Beach" (Sl Aubin sur Mer) on June 10, 1944. The pilot, Lt. John Weese, died in the crash.

Last kiss for the "Smoocher": A P-47 of the 353rd Fighter Group crashed in England during August 1944. The 353rd flew the Thunderbolt until transitioning to the P-51 Mustang in October 1944.

This Thunderbolt crashed and burned on a forward airfield in France on June 21, 1944. Note fragmentation bomb clusters still attached to the starboard wing.

Ground support: P-47 down in the US 12th Armored Division's area of operations during the attack on Würzburg, Germany, April 2, 1945. The pilot was slightly injured in the crash. M-7 "Priest" self-propelled guns are visible in the background.

During the night of June 25, 1944, Japanese holdouts in the area of Aslito airfield on Saipan attacked and damaged or destroyed a number of P-47s of the 318th Fighter Group.

A second view of "Hed-up N' Locked", burnt out on Aslito airfield, Saipan.

Left page, top:
The dangers of landing with a "hung bomb": this P-47 of 389th Fighter Squadron was blown apart when a 500-pound bomb detached while touching down at Asch field in Belgium (USAAF Y-29).

Left page, bottom:
Fire-extinguishing foam covers a Republic P-47 of the 353rd Fighter Group after it crashed at its base in England during September 19, 1943.

Above:
Thunderbolt liberated: troops of the US 35th Infantry Division recovered this 9th Air Force P-47D that had been captured by the Germans. Herne, Germany April 1945.

P-47D "Turnip Termite" of the 387th Fighter Squadron, wrecked in France on June 7, 1944.

A 9th Air Force salvage team recovers "Turnip Termite".

This captured P-47 was found at a Luftwaffe field in Gottingen, Germany during April 1945. The official report describes the Thunderbolt painted olive drab on the fuse-lage, and bright yellow on the belly and tail.

This P-47D of the 353rd Fighter Group suffered a blown tire on its takeoff roll, swerved off the runway and flipped over onto its back. England, April 1944.

The capabilities of USAAF ground crews was unparalleled. Here a P-47 undergoes significant repairs in the primitive environment of a forward field in France, summer 1944.

Maintenance between missions for a P-47 of the 9th Air Force in France, summer 1944. Note the ever helpful M-2 "Cletrac" tractor in the foreground.

A broken back for the "Green Hornet" of the 78th Fighter Group. England 1944.

A P-47 crashed into a headstand on the Marston Matting of a forward airfield in France, during late June 1944.

P-51C of the 383rd Fighter Squadron, bellied in at its 8th Air Force base at Honnington, England, April 1945.

A late war ETO casualty: P-51D "Phyllis" of the 364th Fighter Group, crashed at Honnington, England in early May 1945.

"Lucky Leaky II" a war-weary squadron hack of the 352nd Fighter Squadron, after an engine failure over England on May 2, 1945.

Right page:
Belly wound: the other side of the wreck of P-51C "Lucky Leaky II".

Even the simplest operations can be dangerous: P-51B of the 352nd Fighter Squadron after losing its tail in a taxiing accident at Raydon, England during February 1945.

P-51D of the 78th Fighter Group after a particularly hard landing at Duxford (8th Air Force station F-357) during January 1945.

Shuttle escort: P-51D "Lottie" damaged on landing at Poltava in the USSR during March 1945.

Left page:
Marshmallow Mustang: a P-51D of the 15th Fighter Group, covered in foam on Iwo Jima, March 1945.

"Danny Boy 2" at the end of a ground loop. 353rd Fighter Group in England, December 1944.

P-51C of the 364th Fighter Group crashed at Honnington, England, September 1944. This aircraft is equipped with the British-designed sliding canopy "Malcolm hood" to increase pilot vision.

P-51D of the 21st Fighter Group, crashed on takeoff on a mission from Iwo Jima. Spring 1945.

Left page:
"Miss Jo III", a P-51D of the 78th Fighter Squadron on Iwo Jima, March 10, 1945.

P-51D of the 364th Fighter Group after crash landing at Honnington, England on July 30, 1944.

"Rugged Rebel" of the 364th Fighter Group suffered a loss of power on takeoff from 8th Air Force base at Honnington on October 17, 1944. The aircraft was repaired and put back into service, only to be lost in combat over Holland during February 1945.

Post-war casualty: P-51D "Boogie's Burner" of the 384th Fighter Squadron, upside down at Honnington, May 16, 1945.

P-51D of the 355th Fighter Squadron undergoing repairs at its new base inside the Reich at Ober Olm, Germany (USAAF airfield code Y-64).

Recovering a P-51D of the 307th Fighter Squadron from a wheels-up landing at San Severo, Italy, April 1944.

Right page:
This P-51D of the 364th Fighter Group suffered a landing accident at Honnington, England in October 1944. She was eventually lost in combat in early April 1945.

P-51D engine and cockpit details courtesy of this Mustang wreck of the 364th Fighter Group at Honnington, England during October 1944.

After an oil leak repainted this P-51D of the 82nd Fighter Squadron, the pilot's obscured vision led to a ground loop on January 4, 1945. Quickly repaired and returned to service, this aircraft was lost in combat on February 24, 1945.

P61B "The Spook" of the 548th Night Fighter Squadron crashed into another P-61 while attempting to land on a fogged-in field on Iwo Jima during April 1945.

"Midnite Madness" a P61A of the 548th Night Fighter Squadron battered after a collision on the runway with another Black Widow fighter. Iwo Jima, April 1945.

Douglas A-20B "Lady Jean" of the 47th Bomb Group, damaged by flak and downed at Youks Les Bains, Algeria during late December 1942.

A-20A "Little Hellion", a converted "strafer" of the 89th Bomb Squadron, hit by Japanese flak and crashed at the Seven-Mile Aerodrome near Port Moresby, New Guinea during November 1942. Despite the great need for aircraft in this theater, the aircraft was written off and cannibalized.

A short delay: this A-20 crashed short of the airfield in Nome, Alaska on its lend-lease journey to join the Soviet Air Force. Regardless, it was soon repaired and completed its journey to Russia.

A-20G of the 410th Bomb Group, crashed at Rivenhall, England, on May 9, 1944.

Left page:
Two views of an A-20B of the 47ᵗʰ Bomb
Group down in Algeria in early 1943.

Above:
"Zombia", an A-20G of the 410ᵗʰ Bomb Group down at a
9ᵗʰ Air Force base in France during late December 1944.

Above:
A-20G cracked up at Lancashire, England during October 1944. An interesting view that shows the fuselage bulge necessary to accommodate the twin gun rear turret.

Right page, top:
A-20G "Bill" of the 410th Bomb Group, crashed near a 9th Air Force base in France during November 1944.

Right page, bottom:
A-20G of the 417th Bomb Group, looking very much like a smashed model kit, after a Japanese bombing raid on Mindoro, Philippines during late December 1944. Note the A-20s nose cap, showing details of the .50 caliber gun tubes.

Douglas A-26 Invader of the 89th Attack Squadron bellied in Okinawa, during early August 1945. Note the eight .50 caliber Browning MGs mounted in the nose of this gunship.

"Mischievous Miggs", an A-26 of the 410th Bomb Group, nosed over at a 9th Air Force base in France, April 30, 1945. The A-26 was an advanced aircraft that also served in the Korean and Vietnam wars.

Nose to the grindstone: An A-26 of the 386th Bomb Group, pranged at Beaumont, France on March 9, 1945. Note this is the six-gun (6x .50 caliber MGs) version of the attack bomber.

A-26B of the 386th Bomb Group crashed at St Trond, Belgium during April 1945. Note the .50 caliber MG packs mounted beneath the Invader's wings.

Above:
A-26 of the 386th Bomb Group suffered a landing gear collapse upon landing at its base at Beaumont, France during April 1945. This is the A-26C variant with a glass nose, bombardier position. This aircraft is equipped with underwing gun pods carrying .50 caliber MGs.

Right page, top:
An A-26 gunship of the 386th Bomb Group, crashed at its base at Beaumont, France after a mission on March 11, 1945.

Right page, bottom:
"Lady Marc", an A-26 of the 386th Bomb Group, crashed at St. Trond, Belgium.

B-17s wrecked during the German bombing raid on Poltava, in Soviet territory, on June 21, 1944.

The second shuttle mission (Frantic-2) raiders were tailed to the Soviet base at Poltava. On the evening of June 21, 1944, the Germans bombed the field and destroyed 43 B-17s, damaging 26 more.

Day of Infamy: B-17C Flying Fortress at Hickam Field, blown in half during the Japanese attack on Pearl Harbor, December 7, 1941.

A view of the destroyed B-17 (shown above) from across Hickam Field.

The dangers of handling live ordnance: this badly damaged B-17 was the victim of a bomb-handling accident at its 8th Air Force base in England. May 1943.

B-17F "Bab's Best", part of the 2nd Air Service Group, slid off the taxiway at Meeks Field, Iceland, collapsing the landing gear and causing minor damage. May 1943.

Left page:
The Fortress could take a hit: this B-17G of the 429th Bomb Squadron was nearly cut in half by flak during a mission over Hungary. Despite the horrific damage and three crewmen killed, the aircraft returned to its base in Italy. September 21, 1944.

B-17F of the 303rd Bomb Group made an emergency landing at the 353rd Fighter Group's field at Metfield, England on January 11, 1944. The fighter crews covered her in foamite to minimize the chance of fire.

B-17G of the 401st Bomb Group returned to its base at Watten and suffered a blown tire on landing. The resulting nose-over snapped the inboard port engine. There was no resulting fire – the foamite was applied as a precaution. March 26, 1944.

Japanese photo of a B-17D captured at Clark Field, Luzon, Philippines in early 1942.

B-17 top turret badly damaged by gunfire from a German interceptor.

This B-17 had been captured by the Germans, and was apparently being repaired when it was destroyed in an Allied bombing attack on Chateaufort, France. It was discovered by American troops in September 1944.

Left page:
B-17G "Bonnie Donnie" of the 401st Bomb Group, bellied in at its 8th Air Force base in England. March 5, 1944.

B-17G "Mercy's Madhouse" of the 303rd Bomb Group, right side landing gear collapsed on landing, December 7, 1944

Right page:
B-17G "Sweet Melody" of the 303rd Bomb Group, her return from a mission to Berlin spoiled by this landing accident. May 19, 1944.

Right page, top:
B-17F "Dangerous Dan" of the 379th Bomb Group, crashed in England during December 1943.

Right page, bottom:
B-17F of the 379th Bomb Group, crashed in Overland Farm, Kent during February 1944.

Above:
Nose to tail: B-17s of the 401st Bomb Group collided while taxiing at their 8th Air Force base in England. July 6, 1944.

Rocket attack: this 8th Air Force B-17 had its fuselage ripped open by the explosion of a 21cm rocket launched by a German interceptor. Summer 1943.

B-17G "Hell's Angel" of the 381st Bomb Group, lost part of its nose on a mission over Germany, November 10, 1944. Note the details of the .50 caliber chin turret and cheek guns.

Salvage in the USSR: US air crews recover parts from a Consolidated B-24J Liberator (from the 780th Bomb Group) crashed on Poltava field during one of the Shuttle missions. January, 1945.

B-24J of 780th Bomb Squadron crash landed at Poltava field during early January 1945.

Ploesti survivor: B-24D "The Squaw"
of the 98th Bomb Group, 343rd Bomb
Squadron. A veteran ship, she eventually returned to the USA to participate
in a bond tour.

Right page, top:
"Fearless Fosdick" flies no more. This
B-24 of the 445th Bomb Group was
written off after a landing gear failure
during an emergency landing in Cam-
bridgeshire, August 1944.

Right page, bottom:
Sliding into home: B-24 of the 450th
Bomb Group skids into its base in the
Italian mud. March 1944.

Recovered Liberator: US troops found this German-marked B-24H on the field at Salzburg, Austria. This aircraft (originally from the 732nd Bomb Squadron, 8th Air Force), was used by the German special operations squadron KG200.

Right page:
Bombing the bombers: one of two 7th Air Force B-24s destroyed during a Japanese bombing raid on Funafuti Island, April 22, 1943.

B-24 of the 7th Air Force, crashed during an emergency landing on Makin Island, December 1943.

Left page:
B-24J "Chambermaid" of the 7th Air Force, crashed in the Marianas after a bombing mission against Iwo Jima during September 1944. All of the crew members walked away from the crash.

B-24H "Lonesome Lois" 701st Bomb Squadron, crash landed at RAF station Beccles during July 1944.

B-24J "Shady Lady" of the 715th Bomb Squadron, paid a surprise visit to the RAF Base at Lisset in Yorkshire on November 27, 1944.

Above:
B-24J "Breezy Lady" 458th Bomb Group, 8th Air Force after an emergency landing at an RAF base at Horsham. The pilot expertly landed the big Liberator without the nose wheel, and the aircraft was quickly repaired and returned to service. July, 1944.

Right page:
B-24H "Shack Rat" of the 786th Bomb Squadron, became a total write off after this crash landing at Attlebridge, April 19, 1944.

B-25D of the 38th Bomb Group had the brakes lock on the landing gear and wrecked at Wewak Aerodrome, New Guinea during January, 1943.

This B-25G suffered a blown tire on take-off from its base in China, leading to this wreck in April 1944. Note the 75mm M4 cannon and details of the twin Browning A/N M2 .50 caliber MGs in the nose.

B-25 bellied into a friendly field. India, 1944.

B-25 of the 340th Bomb Group destroyed during a German bombing raid on its base on Corsica during 1944. The fire has consumed most of the Mitchell, but its twin .50 caliber tail guns still remain.

On March 23, 1944, Mount Vesuvius helped the Axis cause as it rained down flaming volcanic ash onto the airfield nearby, damaging several North American B-25s of the 340th Bomb Group.

Above:
B-25J "Angel of Mercy" of the 310th Bomb Group, was hit by flak and lost its hydraulics, forcing a belly landing at Fano airfield in Northern Italy during April 1945.

Right page:
B-25J of the 445th Bomb Squadron, based on Corsica, took a direct hit from flak to its nose, killing the bombardier. The aircraft, a veteran of more than 70 missions, stayed in formation and made it home.

"Little Lady", a veteran Marauder of the 596th Bomb Squadron, 9th Air Force, after an emergency landing at a French base in February 1945.

Left page:
"Hot Pistol" headed for the scrapyard: A Martin B-26B Marauder of the 552nd Bomb Squadron (386th Bomb Group) after a "write-off" crash-landing at Great Dunmow, England during August 1944.

Changing a Pratt & Whitney R-2800 engine on B-26B "Bat Outa Hell" at a Brazilian field. October 1943.

A liberal application of "foamite": this B-26C of the 386th Bomb Group succumbed to battle damage and crashed at Great Dunmow, England during June 1944.

"Blazing Heat" with a broken nose: B-26 Marauder of the 386th Bomb Group made it home to Great Dunmow in one piece, more or less.

Crash scene of the "Crime Doctor": B-26B of the 386th Bomb Group in tatters at Great Dunmow during late July 1944.

Boeing B-29 Superfortress that almost came to a stop on Iwo Jima's short runway. Despite its size limitations for the giant bombers, Iwo Jima was a godsend for the B-29s, offering a safe haven for damaged aircraft unable to make their way back to their base in the Marianas.

Another view of the same B-29, crashed into the embankment on Strip 2 at the Iwo Jima base, April 15, 1945. Note the Cletrac "bomber nurse" attending at the scene of the crash.

On the return flight from a Tokyo raid, this damaged Superfortress put down on the black volcanic ash of Iwo Jima. The invasion fleet can still be seen in the background. March 10, 1945.

This B-29 of the 500th Bomb Group made it all the way home to Saipan only to be wrecked on landing. Spring 1945.

Above:
This B-29 suffered a nose wheel collapse upon return to its base in the CBI.
Note the four-gun forward top turret.

Right page:
B-29 "Gravel Gertie" of the 500th Bomb Group laying in the
dirt on Saipan. August 1945.

125

Above:
B-29 that belly-landed in the ocean after the field at Iwo Jima was fogged in. The crew swam to safety.

Right page:
After a 17-hour mission to Tokyo, this B-29 of the 500th Bomb Group returned to its base on Saipan, only to have a runaway prop completely sever the nose from the fuselage.

e enemy strikes back: a B-29 of the 500th Bomb Group, badly damaged by a Japanese air raid on Saipan, December 7, 1944.